Individuals With Disabilities

The Practicing Administrator's Leadership Series
Jerry J. Herman and Janice L. Herman, Editors

ROADMAPS TO SUCCESS

Other Titles in This Series Include:

The Path to School Leadership
A Portable Mentor
Lee G. Bolman and Terrence E. Deal

Holistic Quality
Managing, Restructuring, and Empowering Schools
Jerry J. Herman

Selecting, Managing, and Marketing Technologies
Jamieson A. McKenzie

Violence in the Schools
How to Proactively Prevent and Defuse It
Joan L. Curcio and Patricia F. First

Women in Administration
Facilitators for Change
L. Nan Restine

Power Learning in the Classroom
Jamieson A. McKenzie

Conflict Resolution
Building Bridges
Neil Katz

Computers: Literacy and Learning
A Primer for Administrators
George E. Marsh II

Restructuring Schools
Doing It Right
Mike M. Milstein

Dealing With Gangs
A Handbook for Administrators
Shirley R. Lal, Dhyan Lal, and Charles M. Achilles

Individuals With Disabilities

Implementing the Newest Laws

Patricia F. First
Joan L. Curcio

CORWIN PRESS, INC.
A Sage Publications Company
Newbury Park, California

For information address:

Corwin Press, Inc.
A Sage Publications Company
2455 Teller Road
Newbury Park, California 91320

SAGE Publications Ltd.
6 Bonhill Street
London EC2A 4PU
United Kingdom

SAGE Publications India Pvt. Ltd.
M-32 Market
Greater Kailash I
New Delhi 110 048 India

Printed in the United States of America

Library of Congress Cataloging-in-Publication Data

First, Patricia F.
  Individuals with disabilities : implementing the newest laws /
Patricia F. First, Joan L. Curcio.
    p.   cm. — (Roadmaps to success)
  Includes bibliographical references.
  ISBN 0–8039–6055–7 (pbk.)
    1. Handicapped children—Education—Law and legislation—United
States. 2. Discrimination against the handicapped—Law and
legislation—United States. 3. Architecture and the physically
handicapped—Law and legislation—United States.   I. Curcio, Joan
L.   II. Title.   III. Series.
  KF4210.F57   1993
  346.7301'3—dc20
  [347.30613]   93–15408

93 94 95 96 10 9 8 7 6 5 4 3 2 1

Corwin Press Production Editor: Marie Louise Penchoen

Contents

Foreword

In *Individuals With Disabilities: Implementing the Newest Laws*, Patricia First and Joan Curcio address the important concerns for educators of complying with the recent equal-access laws in schools. From legal and practical perspectives, they provide clear overviews of the Americans With Disabilities Act (ADA) of 1990 and the Individuals With Disabilities Education Act (IDEA) of 1990, and they show the historical relation of these laws to the earlier, "ground-breaking" laws of the 1970s.

In addition to case law examples and details of provisions and regulations, they analyze the impact of these acts on schools and provide sources for obtaining assistance in complying with their requirements. They also include some wise advice and concrete steps to take for the school administrator faced with compliance concerns. This handbook includes a list of abbreviations common in this specialized area and a well-annotated bibliography.

First and Curcio have put together a valuable guide for all educators who share responsibility for fulfilling the legal requirements of the newest laws concerning individuals with disabilities.

JERRY J. HERMAN
JANICE L. HERMAN
Series Co-Editors

About the Authors

Patricia F. First is Professor of Educational Law and Policy in the Department of Educational Leadership & Policy Studies at the University of Oklahoma, where she conducts policy studies in education related to justice for children, the adequacy of the educational experience, and the preparation of sensitive and knowledgeable educational leaders. She is co-editor of *NOLPE's School Law Reporter*, a member of the Author's Committee of *West's Education Law Reporter*, a member of the Board of Directors of the National Organization on Legal Problems of Education, and an editorial board member for *The International Journal of Educational Reform* and *People and Education*. She is the author of *Educational Policy for School Administrators*, the co-editor of *School Boards: Changing Local Control*, published in the *Contemporary Issues Series* of the National Society for the Study of Education, and the author of numerous articles in policy and practitioner journals. She has been a teacher and administrator in both K-12 and higher education, a policy analyst with both state and federal government, and a National Education Policy Fellow. She earned her B.S. at the University of Massachusetts and her M.S. and Ed.D. at Illinois State University.

Joan L. Curcio is Associate Professor in the Department of Educational Leadership, University of Florida, where she researches and writes on education law—with particular emphasis on advocacy issues—and on school governance—particularly the superintendency. She is also consultant to the Multidisciplinary Diagnostic and Training Program at the University of Florida, a collaborative effort between the Colleges of Medicine and Education to improve the skills of underachieving children. She has had extensive experience as a school practitioner: public school English and journalism teacher, assistant principal, high school principal, and assistant superintendent. She was named among the 100 Top Administrators in North America in 1984 by the National School Boards Association for her work as principal, and she was given the Effie H. Jones Award by FLORIDA AWARE for outstanding contributions to women in educational administration in 1989.

Curcio received her MA from American University, Washington, DC, and her PhD from Virginia Polytechnic and State University, Blacksburg, VA. She presently teaches higher education law, public school law, special education law, and the superintendency and is engaged in research on the beginning superintendency with a group of university researchers from across the country.

Abbreviations

ADA	Americans With Disabilities Act of 1990
ADD	Attention Deficit Disorder
ADHD	Attention Deficit and Hyperactivity Disorder
AIDS	Acquired Immune Deficiency Syndrome
BIA	Bureau of Indian Affairs
CASE	Council of Administrators of Special Education, Inc.
EAHCA	Education of All Handicapped Children Act
EEOC	Equal Employment Opportunities Commission
EHA	Education of All Handicapped Children Act
EHCA	Education of All Handicapped Children Act
FAPE	Free Appropriate Public Education
FCC	Federal Communications Commission
IDEA	Individuals With Disabilities Education Act of 1990
IEP	Individualized Educational Program or Individual Education Plan
LEA	Local Education Agency or Local Education Authority
LRE	Least Restrictive Environment
NASSP	National Association of Secondary School Principals
PL	Public Law
SEA	State Education Agency or State Education Authority
SED	Severely Emotionally Disturbed

Equal Access: The Letter and the Spirit

Since the early 1970s, the United States has moved steadily in the direction of increased inclusionary policy and law for persons with disabilities. In the field of education, this reform movement has been known by several names—*special education integration, full inclusion,* and *the regular education initiative.* These terms suggest the motivation for this reform, that it is desirable in the eyes of parents and education professionals to educate all students in the same schools and the same classes to the maximum extent possible. The feeling is that segregation denies special students equal educational opportunity (Schattman & Benay, 1992).

The most recent extension of this movement, the Americans With Disabilities Act of 1990 (ADA), took effect on July 26, 1992, for public and private employers of 25 or more persons. This law protects persons with disabilities, persons who were formerly disabled, and persons perceived as disabled. The ADA also protects persons who are suffering discrimination resulting from a relationship with a disabled person.

School districts should have by now taken steps to comply with the ADA's anti-discrimination and affirmative action provisions.

However, compliance with this law will be an evolving process. The standard for compliance with the law's basic provisions is a flexible concept called *reasonable accommodation*. During the next few years, unfolding case law will add a body of interpretation to this and other concepts inherent in the ADA and in the Individuals With Disabilities Education Act of 1990 (IDEA). The purpose of this book is to provide educators with an overview of the newest laws concerning individuals with disabilities. We start with two important caveats.

First, interpretive case law concerning these statutes is being decided almost daily. Therefore, when confronted with new or unusual circumstances related to the inclusion and/or accommodation of persons with disabilities, the educator should consult with the school district's attorney immediately.

Second, and more important, we strongly believe that in the schools the spirit of this law should be firmly upheld. Children with disabilities have been met with exclusion and discrimination for too long in the nation's schools. We offer the information and suggestions that follow in the hope that they may guide educators to make their schools models of justice for children with disabilities and model workplaces for adults with disabilities. Only then will our educational system live up to the spirit of the ADA, the IDEA, and their ground-breaking predecessors, the Education for All Handicapped Children Act of 1974 and the Rehabilitation Act of 1973.

Each of these acts, including the newest, the ADA, has expanded federal protection of the civil rights of persons with disabilities. The ADA was enacted "to establish a clear and comprehensive prohibition of discrimination on the basis of disability" (Public Law 101-336, 104 STAT.327). The ADA attempts to provide clear, strong, consistent, and enforceable standards prohibiting discrimination against individuals with disabilities, without respect to their age, nature of disability, or extent of disability" (Turnbull, 1990, p. 6).

Over 43 million Americans suffer from one or more physical or mental disabilities. This number is expected to increase as our society ages. Until recently these individuals have been removed or segregated from the mainstream of society, and despite some areas of improvement, many forms of discrimination still occur, even in critical areas, such as employment and education. Data show that "people with disabilities, as a group, occupy an inferior status in our society." They are "a discrete and insular minority" with a history of "purposeful unequal treatment and political powerlessness" who are viewed with many stereotypical assumptions (Public Law 101-336, 104 STAT.329).

Prior to the enactment of the Americans With Disabilities Act, individuals with disabilities who were victims of discrimination had no legal recourse. Congress felt that "the continuing existence of unfair and unnecessary discrimination and prejudice denied people with disabilities the opportunity to compete on an equal basis and to pursue those opportunities for which our free society is justifiably famous" (Public Law 101-336, 104 STAT.329). Now, the force of law is helping every person have a chance at those opportunities—beginning with their education.

Americans With Disabilities Act of 1990

Purpose of the Statute

The Americans With Disabilities Act of 1990 (ADA) is the first law concerning individuals with disabilities that has had a large impact on schools. The purpose of the ADA is (1) to provide a clear and comprehensive national mandate for the elimination of discrimination against individuals with disabilities; (2) to provide clear, strong, consistent, enforceable standards addressing discrimination against individuals with disabilities; (3) to ensure that the federal government plays a central role in enforcing the standards established in the Act on behalf of individuals with disabilities; and (4) to invoke the sweep of congressional authority, including the power to enforce the 14th Amendment and to regulate commerce, in order to address the major areas of discrimination faced day to day by individuals with disabilities.

Legislative Background

The Americans With Disabilities Act derives its substance from Section 504 of the Rehabilitation Act of 1973, but its procedure is based on Title 7 of the Civil Rights Act of 1964.

Finding that Americans with disabilities faced an inordinate number of inequities, President Reagan created the National Council on Disabilities to study the problem and make recommendations for improvement to Congress. After more than 3 years of research, the council wrote and passed to Congress in 1988 Public Law (or PL) 101-336, what is now known as the ADA. Congressional inaction stalled the bill until well into the Bush presidency despite his strong support. The final version was not approved until July 13, 1990.

Definitions of Terms

The following definitions may assist administrators as they attempt to interpret and implement the Act:

- A *"qualified individual with a disability"* is an individual with a disability who, with or without reasonable accommodation, can perform the essential functions of the job that the individual holds or desires (PL 101-336).
- "A *reasonable accommodation* [italics added] includes making existing facilities used by employees readily accessible to and usable by individuals with disabilities; job restructuring, part-time or modified work schedules, reassignments to vacant positions, acquisition or modification of equipment or devices, appropriate adjustment or modifications of examinations and training materials or policies, the provision of qualified readers or interpreters, and other similar accommodations" (Turnbull, 1990, p. 8).
- "*Undue hardship* [italics added] on the employer is a significant difficulty or expense when considered in light of the nature and cost of accommodation, the overall financial resources of the facility or facilities involved, the number of persons employed at the facility, the effect on expenses and resources or the impact on the operation of the facility, the overall financial resources of the employer, the size of the business with respect to the number of its employees, the number, type, and location of its facilities, and the type of operation" (Turnbull, 1990, p. 8).
- Discrimination consists of denying participation in programs and operations, denying participation of unequal benefit,

offering only separate benefits, and not offering programs and operations in integrated settings (Turnbull, 1990).

- *Alternative methods of service* for non-accessible public accommodations are considered *readily achievable* if they are accomplishable and able to be carried out without much difficulty or expense. Factors to be considered include "the nature and cost of the action required, the overall financial resources and size of the facility and the covered entity, including the impact of compliance on the facility's or entity's expenses, resources, and operations, and the type of operation carried on by the entity" (Turnbull, 1990, p. 11).

Major Provisions

The Americans With Disabilities Act is very broad legislation aimed at protecting the rights of all disabled persons in a wide range of situations (National Association of Secondary School Principals [NASSP], 1992, February), including private sector employment, availability of public services and services provided by state and local governments, access to public accommodations (for example, theaters, hotels, restaurants, shopping centers, and grocery stores), public and private transportation services, and telecommunications relay services (for the hearing impaired).

Protected Individuals (Conditions Covered)

The following persons and circumstances are covered under the Act:

- Individuals with disabilities as the term is defined under Sec. 504: a person who has, has a history of having, or is regarded as having an impairment that significantly limits one or more of life's major functions.
- The Act prohibits discrimination against an individual who has successfully completed a supervised drug rehabilitation program and is no longer using illegal drugs.
- The Act allows testing for illegal drugs, but prohibits discrimination against users of illegal drugs if they are otherwise entitled to health services or other services related to drug rehabilitation.

- Persons with AIDS are covered, but persons with a contagious disease or infection may be excluded or denied a job or benefit if there exists a significant risk of transmitting the infection to others through its receipt and if reasonable accommodations cannot eliminate such risk.
- Persons who oppose any act or practice made unlawful by this Act, and persons who enjoy rights guaranteed by this Act, are protected from retaliation or intimidation regarding the Act (PL 101-336).

SEA/LEA Requirements

Procedures for locating, identifying, and evaluating all children who have or are suspected of having a disability should be in place in each state. This "child find" responsibility applies to children from birth to age 21. Evaluations of potential recipients of special education and related services should be conducted promptly. The ADA is only enforceable by private individuals. There are no funds for federal investigation of compliance (Parrino, 1992).

Conditions and Individuals Not Protected

Homosexuality, bisexuality, transvestitism, pedophilia, transsexualism, exhibitionism, voyeurism, gender identity disorders or other sexual behavior disorders, compulsive gambling, kleptomania, pyromania, and psychoactive substance use disorders resulting from current illegal use of drugs are not impairments and are not disabilities under the Act (Turnbull, 1990).

As used in the Act, the term *employer* does not include the United States, corporations wholly owned by the government of the United States or an Indian tribe, and tax-exempt private membership clubs (other than labor organizations) (PL 101-336).

Specific Titles

Title 1. Employment

Discrimination in employment is prohibited. Covered employment practices include application procedures, hiring, advancement, discharge, compensation, job training, and other conditions of employment. The rules on employment discrimination do not apply to religious organizations and small businesses (fewer than 25 employees until 1994, and 15 or fewer employees after 1994). It is permissible under the Act for religious organizations to give preference in employment to members of a particular sect and for such organizations to require all applicants and employees to conform to the organization's religious tenets (PL 101-336).

What Should School Districts Do?

Job descriptions should be reviewed to ensure that the desired qualifications reflect the essential job functions. Inquiries regarding physical or mental disabilities should be removed from employment applications. All individuals involved in applicant selection should be aware of their duties and responsibilities under the Americans With Disabilities Act. Employment testing should be reviewed for relevance to the essential job functions. Medical examinations, where legally acceptable, should be collected and maintained in a file separate from the applicant file and should be treated as confidential medical records. A formal grievance procedure should be adopted and published, and at least one employee should be designated to coordinate these efforts. This employee's name, office address, and telephone number should be made available to all employees.

Title 2. Public Services

The Act prohibits discrimination in programs, activities, and services provided by state and local governments and their instrumentalities regardless of whether they receive federal funds. Private clubs and religious organizations are exempt.

What Should School Districts Do?

Furnish appropriate aids to afford disabled individuals equal opportunities to participate in available programs and services. Give primary consideration to requests made by the disabled individual. Ensure that individuals with impaired hearing or vision receive pertinent information about available programs and services.

Title 3. Public Accommodations and Services Operated by Public Entities

The Act prohibits discrimination in public accommodations and services provided by the private sector, including transportation. Transportation by school bus of school children, personnel, and equipment to and from a public elementary or secondary school and school-related activities is covered under the Act. Fixed-route transportation systems (including school bus routes) should provide service to individuals with disabilities (including wheelchair users) that is comparable to the service provided to individuals without disabilities.

Reasonable changes in policies, practices, and procedures must be made to avoid discrimination. This includes providing auxiliary aids and services to vision- or hearing-impaired individuals and removing physical barriers. If barriers cannot be removed, alternative methods of providing services must be available, if readily achievable. All new construction and alterations must be handicap-accessible. Special care should be taken in considering alterations that could effect access to an area of any facility that contains a primary function such as bathrooms, telephones, and water fountains. Private clubs and religious organizations are exempt.

What Should School Districts Do?

Post directions to accessible facilities at all inaccessible entrances. Use the international symbol for accessibility at all appropriate entrances. If structural changes are required, a transition plan for making such changes should have been in place prior to July 26, 1992. Elevators are not required in schools that are less than three stories or have less than 3,000 square feet per story. Be sure that the district can provide proper transportation to and from school and school activities for all students, regardless of disabling conditions.

Title 4. Telecommunications

This title amends the Telecommunications Act of 1934 by adding a section that authorizes the Federal Communications Commission (FCC) to establish minimum standards for telecommunications and relay services for hearing- and speech-impaired individuals.

All telecommunications services must offer relay services for hearing- and speech-impaired individuals and must provide closed-captioning of public service announcements.

What Should School Districts Do?

Ensure that communications for individuals with disabilities are as effective as communications for nondisabled individuals.

Title 5. Miscellaneous Provisions

The Americans With Disabilities Act replaces the word *handicapped* with *disabled* and the word *qualified* with the phrase *otherwise qualified*. It also allows complainants to claim discrimination "because of" the disability as opposed to "solely by reason of the handicap." In addition, the ADA makes no requirement that the program or entity in question must have received federal funds.

The ADA does not invalidate or limit the remedies, rights, and procedures of any federal law or law of any state or political subdivision of any state or jurisdiction that provides greater or equal protection for the rights of individuals with disabilities than are afforded by the ADA (PL 101-336). Nothing in the Act should be construed to apply a lesser standard than Title 5 of the Rehabilitation Act of 1973 (Gordon, 1991).

Nothing in the Act requires an individual with a disability to accept an accommodation, aid, service, opportunity, or benefit. Nothing in the Act precludes the prohibition or restriction of smoking in areas covered by Titles 1, 2, or 3 (Gordon, 1991).

Districts are required, by July 26, 1993, to complete a self-evaluation of compliance with the Americans With Disabilities Act. The evaluation is limited to those policies and practices not included in any self-evaluation conducted pursuant to Section 504. An opportunity for participation must be made available for all interested persons, disabled and nondisabled. The self-evaluation file, consisting of a list of all interested persons who participated, a description of areas examined and problems identified, and a description of any modifications made, must be kept for 3 years following the conclusion of the evaluation.

Enforcement and Remedies

- Alternative Dispute Resolution is encouraged but not required by the Americans With Disabilities Act.
- The insurance industry is exempt from the provisions of the ADA.
- Under the 11th Amendment, states are not immune from lawsuits filed under the ADA.
- Employment:
  Complaints may be filed with the EEOC; appeals may be taken to court.
  Remedies include back pay and court orders to stop discrimination.
- Public Services:
  Complaints may be filed with federal agencies designated by the attorney general, or complainants may bring private lawsuits.
  Remedies include recovery of actual damages and court orders prohibiting further discrimination.
- Public Accommodations:
  Individuals may seek court orders prohibiting discrimination (monetary damages may not be obtained); complaints may be filed with the attorney general, who may file a lawsuit to stop discrimination and to obtain monetary damages and penalties.
- Transportation:
  Complaints may be filed with the Department of Transportation, or private lawsuits may be brought.
- Telecommunications:
  Complaints may be filed with the FCC.
- Attorneys' fees may be recovered by any individual who prevails in any complaint or lawsuit against an ADA-covered entity.

Impact of the Americans With Disabilities Act

- "It will save the nation billions of dollars over coming years in public and private funds now spent ostensibly to 'help' people with disabilities, but effectively keeping them dependent on society's largess" (Parrino, 1992, p. 66).

- The new role of schools is to prepare students with disabilities to take full advantage of the new opportunities available in employment; to participate in and use public accommodations (using more community-based and community-referenced-curriculum); to provide all students with disabilities instruction on the use of public transportation (regardless of the nature or extent of the disability); and to provide instruction on the use of telecommunications systems (Turnbull, 1990).

- Senator Tom Harkin of Iowa expressed the dream of the Americans With Disabilities Act: "With the passage of the Americans With Disabilities Act, we as a society make a pledge that every child with a disability will have the opportunity to maximize his or her potential to live proud, productive, and prosperous lives in the mainstream of our society" (Quoted in Turnbull, 1990).

- Much of what is included in the ADA has been covered previously in the EAHCA, the Rehabilitation Act, and Section 504. However, the operation and administration of schools is directly impacted by Title 1, the employment section, and Title 2, the programs, activities, and services section. Under Title 1, employment decisions made by schools may not discriminate against a current employee or applicant if she or he is a "qualified individual with a disability." An individual is "qualified" if she or he can perform the essential functions of the job with or without reasonable accommodation. Title 1 became effective for school districts with more than 25 employees on July 26, 1992.

- It is not the intent of the ADA to place undue hardships on existing programs, services, or employers; hardship exemptions are available for specific situations. For instance, school districts are not required to retrofit all existing facilities. Redesign of equipment, reassignment of services to accessible buildings, provision of aids, and installation of elevators or chair lifts are all acceptable methods of achieving accessibility. Administrators are cautioned, however, that physically carrying an individual with a disability is considered an ineffective and unacceptable method. School districts should choose the method that will provide services in the most integrated appropriate setting (Long, n.d.).

- Under Title 2, schools must operate programs and services that are readily accessible to and usable by individuals with disabilities. This includes making reasonable accommodations. Also, the programs and services must be provided in an integrated setting, and eligibility standards or rules that deny disabled individuals access to programs and services must be eliminated. However, it is not the intent of the Act to cause school districts to make fundamental alterations in programs and services.
- In disciplining children with disabilities who are using illegal drugs or alcohol, educational agencies may use their regular disciplinary procedures, applicable to all students, and are not required to use the due process procedures of the EHA and the Individuals With Disabilities Education Act (Turnbull, 1990).

Where to Go for Help or Additional Information

The *Job Accommodation Network* (800-526-7234) is a valuable resource for schools that are trying to make reasonable accommodations without excessive costs. If demands are made for accommodations or inclusion of conditions that administrators believe are unreasonable, clarification of the law's requirements may be obtained through the *Office of the US Attorney General* at 202-514-0301 or the *EEOC* at 202-663-4903 (NASSP, 1992, February). The EEOC can also be reached at 800-USA-EEOC (Cape, 1992).

The *ADA Watch Hotline* provides information to those trying to comply with the law and works to identify those who refuse. Barriers encountered in public places and other problems/concerns may be reported to them at 800-875-7814 (both voice and TDD) (Parrino, 1992).

Individuals With Disabilities
Education Act of 1990

The purpose of the Individuals With Disabilities Education Act (IDEA) remains the same as the Education of All Handicapped Children Act (EAHCA), the revolutionary statute passed by Congress in 1974. That purpose is to assure that children with disabilities have access to a free appropriate education and equal educational opportunity. Under the law, states must have a plan to ensure that children with disabilities are identified, located, and evaluated and that an Individual Education Plan (IEP) is developed for each child so identified.

In October 1990, the Education of All Handicapped Children Act (Public Law 94-142) was amended by Public Law 101-476, and the name was changed to the Individuals With Disabilities Education Act. The term *handicapped student* and similar uses of *handicap* were changed to read "child/student/individual with a disability." This change reflected the desire of individuals with disabilities and others to indicate that a disability is simply one aspect of a person.

The new amendments added autism and traumatic brain injury to the categories of students eligible for special education and related services; addressed new discretionary programs for transition and special education services and minority outreach; augmented definitions; addressed Native American services and students with attention deficit disorders (ADD); and allowed private citizens to bring suit against states and state and local education agencies.

Major Provisions

In passing the IDEA into law, Congress clearly intended that the rights of persons with disabilities be enumerated in clear and unequivocal fashion. The major provisions of the IDEA are as follows:

Federal Assistance

Federal financial assistance is provided to states that develop an appropriate plan for identifying and educating children with disabilities.

The IEP

The Individual Education Plan (IEP) that is to be developed for every child is an integral part of the IDEA. The IEP should be developed cooperatively with the student's parents or guardian and the appropriate school officials, and it should identify the educational needs of the child and specify the services that will be provided to meet those needs.

Procedural Safeguards

The following procedural safeguards are specified by the Act to protect the rights of the disabled child and his or her parents:

1. Parents have access to all relevant records with respect to the identification, evaluation, and educational placement of their child.
2. Parents have the opportunity to obtain their own independent educational evaluation of their child.
3. Both administrative and judicial review of a placement decision are available.

4. Parents are entitled to an impartial due process hearing before the state or local education agency if they object to the child's IEP.
5. The decision of a local hearing officer may be appealed to the state education agency.
6. The final administrative decision may be contested in a civil action in state or federal court.

The Stay-Put Provision

The Act has a "stay-put" provision that leaves the student in the current (usually public) educational placement during the course of review proceedings. If parents choose, they may remove their child to another (private) placement, but they do so at their own financial risk. Reimbursement is only possible after the fact if the private placement is found to be appropriate and the placement decision of the district is found to be inappropriate.

Students may be placed in private schools, at public expense, if an appropriate public placement in unavailable. Such placement, when decided by the district, is at no cost to the parent or guardian.

Least Restrictive Environment: Mainstreaming

Students with disabilities should be educated in the least restrictive environment (LRE). LRE is a primary consideration of the courts in placement disputes between parents and school districts. Because placement decisions are made on an individual basis, it is difficult for the courts to provide specific guidelines; however, some general directions are available.

To be in compliance with this mandate, states should establish procedures that assure that children with disabilities are educated with nondisabled students "to the maximum extent possible and that removal of children with disabilities from the regular educational setting occurs only when the nature or severity of the disability is such that education in regular classes with the use of supplementary aids and services cannot be achieved satisfactorily" (Osborne, 1992, p. 369). The phrase "maximum extent possible" hints that there is no concrete set of qualifications for the decision regarding whether and to what extent a student should be mainstreamed. Case law, however, indicates that the mandate of LRE is secondary to the provision of appropriate services. The "maximum extent" changes depending on the individual situation (Osborne, 1992).

The Eighth Circuit, for example, has held that public school placements are always less restrictive than private placements, even though the public school placement may mean less contact with nondisabled students. Mainstreaming is seen by the courts as one component of an appropriate education, but it is not the most important component. That distinction is given to the provision of necessary special education services (Osborne, 1992).

There is an obvious tension between these two provisions (mainstreaming and appropriate services for the individual), and the IDEA "does not provide any substantive standards for finding the proper balance" (Osborne, 1992, p. 374). It may be beneficial for districts to consider the following two-part test used by some courts to determine IDEA compliance:

1. Is education in the regular classroom, with supplementary aids and services, satisfactorily achievable?
2. If the answer to Part 1 is no, has the school mainstreamed the child to the maximum extent possible?

In determining the answers to these questions, districts (and courts) should consider "the child's ability to grasp the regular education curriculum, the nature and severity of the disability, the effect the child's presence would have on the functioning of the regular class, the child's overall experience in the mainstream, and the amount of exposure the child would have to nondisabled students" (Osborne, 1992, p. 375).

Mainstreaming has been defined as "the concept of serving the handicapped within the regular school program, with support personnel and services, rather than placing children in self-contained special classes" (Osborne, 1990, p. 445).

The following options are examples of mainstreaming:

1. Student remains in the regular classroom all day and receives special instruction from a traveling special education teacher.

2. Student is based in the regular classroom but leaves to receive services in a special education resource room.
3. Student receives the major portion of his or her education in a special education class, but joins other students for non-academic activities.
4. Student's disability is so severe that no mainstreaming is attempted. (Osborne, 1990)

ADD and the IDEA

Students diagnosed with attention deficit disorder (ADD) must be found to have one or more specified physical or mental impairments and must be found to require special education and related services by reason of one or more of these impairments in order to be eligible under Part B of the IDEA. Services must be designed to meet their unique needs in view of the diagnosis of ADD.

Although ADD is not specifically listed, it does fall under Part B protections under the category of Other Health Impaired in cases where ADD adversely affects learning ability and school performance.

ADD students may also be eligible under the Specific Learning Disability and Seriously Emotionally Disturbed categories.

Children with ADD or Attention Deficit and Hyperactivity Disorder (ADHD) must be provided with a free appropriate public education (FAPE). The rights and protections of the IDEA should be extended to these children and their parents; however, a medical diagnosis of ADD alone is not sufficient to render a child eligible for services under Part B. A final determination of the need for services should be made by a multidisciplinary team, including at least one teacher or other specialist with knowledge in the area of suspected disability.

Medically Fragile Children and Related Services

Medically fragile children are defined as "those children in need of both a medical device to compensate for the loss of a vital body function and substantial and ongoing nursing care to avert death or further disability" (Greismann, 1990, p. 403). Local education agencies (LEAs) are not required to provide medical services, that is, those services normally provided by a licensed physician, except for diagnostic or evaluation purposes.

LEAs are having difficulty differentiating between "related services," required by the IDEA, and "medical services," excluded under the IDEA. Teachers are concerned that they may be asked to perform services that they are neither trained for nor comfortable with.

For example, in *Tatro* (*Irving Independent School District v. Tatro*, 1984), a case decided under the Education for All Handicapped Children Act, the Supreme Court held that clean intermittent catheterization was a "related service." The school district was required to provide this service for the child during school hours, as a related and supportive educational service required to assist the child to benefit from an education. It was clear to the Court that without having catheterization services provided to her, this student could not have attended school and, therefore, could not have benefited from special education. Another element in this case was that medical personnel are not required for the performance of clean intermittent catheterization. In its decision, the Court established a three-part test for determining which services are "related" and which are "medical."

When confronted with such a question, districts should ask:

1. Is the child disabled so as to require special education and related services?
2. Is the service necessary for the child to benefit from special education?
3. Can the service be provided by someone other than a physician?

In cases such as *Detsel* (*Detsel v. Board of Education of the Auburn Enlarged City School District*, 1987), where services do not fall solidly under either of the two categories (related or medical), the category definition that more closely resembles the requested services should be used. There is no clear-cut standard for these cases. Also, districts should be aware that if medical personnel are needed, other sources of payment may be available. For example, in the *Detsel* case it was held that a student was entitled to obtain Medicaid payments for private-duty nursing services provided while attending a public school.

Case Law Concerned With Least Restrictive Environment

The courts have given some guidelines to the educator for making decisions regarding the least restrictive environment.

- In *Briggs* (*Briggs v. Board of Education of the State of Connecticut*, 1989), the court decided that the presumption in favor of mainstreaming must be weighed against the importance of providing an appropriate education to handicapped students.
- In *Barnett* (*Barnett v. Fairfax County School Board*, 1989), the court ruled that placing students in centralized special education programs as opposed to programs located in their neighborhood school does not violate the IDEA, in spite of the preference to educate special education students in the schools they would attend if not disabled.
- In *Gilette* (*Gilette v. Fairland Board of Education*, 1989) and *Lisio* (*Lisio v. Woodland Hills School District*, 1989), the court ruled that the LRE is not required when the specialized instruction needed by a student would pose a considerable disruption to the regular class and a decreased educational benefit to the student.

School officials and judges now have a road map to guide them in making placement decisions. Very simply, the total educational program must first confer an educational benefit on the handicapped child. Second, when appropriate, it must provide the handicapped child with opportunities for mainstreaming to the maximum extent appropriate.

The "Due Weight" Standard

Even in the most careful district there will be challenges and appeals. When this happens, courts are required to give "due weight" (consideration to an appropriate degree) to decisions of Level 1 hearing officers. Because these officers are often district-level administrators, it is important to note the way that courts look at these initial decisions.

The courts will (1) examine the way the hearing officer arrived at the administrative decision and (2) consider the original findings to be prima facie correct. In other words, the decision as made will prevail until contradicted and overcome by other evidence. "If the findings were made in a regular manner and with evidentiary support, they are entitled to presumptive validity" (Menacker, 1992, p. 14). Attending to this "regular manner," that is, to the correctness of the process, is very important for the district. Each step in a procedure and the reasons for each decision made must be thoroughly documented. If the court finds the hearing officer in error, he or she must explain the decision.

Remedies

Before filing a suit, a party should exhaust administrative remedies (*Harper v. School Administrative District No. 37*, 1989). The courts are concerned with factual accuracy and administrative efficiency, but they are equally concerned with local school autonomy and the conservation of judicial resources. The exhaustion-of-remedies rule is meant to keep cases from coming to court, if they can be resolved administratively.

The "futility exception" remains for use in several categories, including (1) denial of an administrative hearing by the LEA (*Ezratty v. Commonwealth of Puerto Rico*, 1983), (2) the possibility of severe harm to the student (*Phipps v. New Hanover County Board of Education*, 1982) , and (3) a situation in which adequate relief is not available administratively (*J. G. v. Rochester City*, 1987).

A reviewing court may hold a hearing admitting all prior evidence and any new evidence offered and make a decision based on the preponderance of the evidence (*Roncker v. Walter*, 1983), but due weight must be given to the original decision.

Two inquiries are made during the review. The first is to investigate whether procedural requirements have been met by the state or district; the second is to review whether the student's IEP and placement provide the opportunity for educational benefit (*Hendrick Hudson District Board of Education v. Rowley*, 1982).

Districts need to accommodate parents' wishes in the hearing processes whenever possible to fulfill both the spirit of the law and the court interpretations. For example, parents may request that a due process hearing be closed if the hearing will involve sensitive issues (*Webster Groves School District v. Pulitzer Publishing Company,* 1990). Also, parents with a hearing or other physical disability that prevents their full participation in a student's IEP conference may tape record the conference without violating the rights of the LEA or its teachers (*E. H. v. Tirozzi,* 1990).

Courts may dismiss a parent's complaint if the parent refuses to participate in any part of an administrative or judicial hearing (*Nathaniel L. v. Exeter School District,* 1990).

Acceptable Suits/Recovery of Damages

Damages will probably not be recovered in a combined EHA/504 claim if both claims have identical facts and origins (*Burke County Board of Education v. Denton,* 1990), although some courts will allow injunctive relief for one and damages for the other (*Begay v. Hodel,* 1990). Suit may also be filed (under Sec. 1983 of the Civil Rights Act) for a violation of equal protection or due process rights under the 14th Amendment. The result of such a suit may be damages and/or an injunction (*Begay v. Hodel,* 1990).

A plaintiff is allowed to sue and seek relief under all three statutes simultaneously (*Joseph P. v. Ambach,* 1982), with the following limitations. In order to recover under Sec. 1983 when suing under the Individuals With Disabilities Education Act, plaintiffs must show that the school or state committed a constitutional violation beyond the violation of the IDEA (*Edward B. v. Paul,* 1987). In a 504 case, a plaintiff must prove only that the defendant's action had a disparate impact or effect that implies some amount of intent to discriminate (*Alexander v. Choate,* 1985). Mere negligence is not a reason for recovery under Sec. 1983 or 504 (*Daniels v. Williams,* 1986).

Students or parents who prevail in a suit under the IDEA, Sec. 504 or Sec. 1983, have the right to recover attorney's fees. Although recovery is possible under any or all of these statutes, courts discourage the filing of multiple-claim suits and tend to limit damages under Sec. 504 and Sec. 1983 if the suit is essentially based on the IDEA. Parents seeking recovery of attorney's fees are required to claim them and to inform the school district of such a claim (*Rapid City School District 51-4 v. Vahle*, 1990). If a settlement is reached, the fees recovered must be for work performed prior to the settlement (*Barlow/Gresham Union High School District No. 2 v. Mitchell*, 1989).

In order to prevail, the "parent's action must cause the defendant school or state to take some action to satisfy the parent's demand" (Turnbull, 1990, p. 42). The degree of this success affects the size of the recovery. Size of the award is based on the attorney's time and labor, the customary fee, the amount of money involved in the case, the attorney's results, and his or her experience and ability (*Digre v. Independent School District No. 623*, 1990).

Tuition may be recovered if a parent can show that the LEA placement was not appropriate. This may be done even if the placement was made without exhausting administrative remedies under the IDEA; however, the outcome is not assured. The LEA must be notified of the placement and given an opportunity to correct or replace its programs or placements. The parents must then file a due process hearing or suit seeking reimbursement annually. If the parents prove that the private program is appropriate and the LEA program is not, they may recover damages in the form of reimbursement for tuition and other educational expenses (*Doe v. Smith*, 1988).

Does the District Have Rights?

Districts have the following resources at their disposal for limiting parental conduct in IDEA cases (Osborne, 1992):

1. Parents rights are not absolute.
2. Courts may reduce the amount of attorney's fees that parents may recover if the parents unreasonably prolong the final resolution of the controversy.
3. Parents who show a "clearly vexatious" posture may be required to pay attorney's fees to the school district.
4. Defendant education agencies may seek court sanctions against parents or their attorney. Two qualifications need emphasis:

a. The case must be found devoid of merit, and the purpose of the case must be improper (harassment or unreasonable delay).

b. The right of a free appropriate public education for the child with disabilities is always paramount.

Current Case Law

Regarding undue parental hostility in IDEA cases, the Seventh Circuit has ruled that parental hostility is a "permissible . . . part of the educational benefit calculation" (Zirkel, 1992, p. 5) in IDEA placement disputes. The court felt that barring consideration of parental attitudes "would, in effect, be punishing the children for the actions of their parents" (Zirkel, 1992, p. 4).

This holding, although disturbing to professional educators, is bounded in several ways. First, the ruling was very close, and it may not spread beyond the Seventh Circuit. Second, parental hostility was treated "as a factor, not the factor in determining the appropriateness of an IEP" (Zirkel, 1992, p. 5). Third, the ruling is "limited to prospective evaluations of an IEP" (Zirkel, 1992, p. 5), and the "reasonably calculated" educational benefit test is applied to the school's efforts, not the parents' attitudes.

It is generally accepted that parents' attitudes toward their children's education are a major factor in the children's overall achievement. Parents who are supportive of schools and their programs are more likely to take an active roll in the educational process. Children sense the importance of the educational endeavor and respond accordingly.

Conversely, children whose parents oppose a particular program or placement are likely to be exposed to many negative feelings and comments about education and to begin to view the educational process as adversarial or hostile. When such parents cannot be convinced to work with a prescribed program, courts must consider whether the child will be able to benefit from the placement.

In *Burlington* (*Burlington School Committee v. Massachusetts Department of Education*, 1985), the court held that in a case where a court determines that a private placement desired by the parents was proper under the Act and that an IEP calling for placement in a public school was inappropriate, reimbursement to parents is available even though their unilateral decision to place their child in a private school violates the stay-put provision. Such reimbursement is limited, however, to cases in which the parents prevail in court, and even in these cases, full reimbursement is not automatic. Consideration is given to the attempt by all parties to cooperate in coming to a final placement decision.

Burlington answered many of the concerns surrounding parents' unilateral placement of their children in private schools, but it did not address the question of placement in non-approved private settings. This question was answered by the Second Circuit in *Tucker* (*Tucker v. Bay Shore Union Free School District*, 1989) and the Fourth Circuit in *Carter* (*Carter v. Florence County School District Four*, 1992). At present there is a large schism between the two courts as to what types of unilateral placement decisions by parents can be reimbursed.

The Second Circuit held that placement of a child in a non-approved private school violates the requirement that placements meet the standards of the state educational agency. The Fourth Circuit, in contrast, interpreted congressional intent to mean that a private school would have to meet state educational standards only when the child is placed in the private school by the state or local school system. They held that there was simply no requirement that the private school be approved by the state in parent-placement reimbursement cases. The final decision on this matter will now have to be left to the Supreme Court.

Amendments and Modifications

ADD and the IDEA

Attention deficit disorder (ADD) has not been included as a separate category in the Individuals With Disabilities Education Act because students with ADD are eligible for services under the Act if the student's disorder is defined as a chronic or acute health problem resulting in limited alertness. ADD-diagnosed students identified for services must be provided with an appropriate IEP.

The following changes were made to the Education of the Handicapped Act in 1990 with the enactment of PL 101-476:

Expanded Categories: Autism and Traumatic Brain Injury

Students with autism (defined as "a developmental disability that significantly affects verbal and nonverbal communication and social interaction") and traumatic brain injury (defined as "an open or closed brain injury caused by external force or internal occurrence but not the result of birth trauma or degenerative disease") whose resulting impairments adversely affect educational performance are included as "children with disabilities."

Related Services: Therapeutic Recreation and Social Work Services

Therapeutic recreation and social work services and rehabilitation counseling are all included as related services. Some courts resist charging the schools with essentially psychotherapeutic services, but it is not uniformly true that courts will interpret the related services provisions conservatively (Turnbull, 1990).

Transition Services

Transition services (services necessary to move from school to postschool) should aim toward preparing students with disabilities for independent living, full participation in community programs, and use of assistive technology devices and services. A statement regarding these services must be included in a student's IEP beginning no later than the student's 16th birthday (or earlier when appropriate). The statement should include a list of the transition services the student will need prior to leaving school. The LEA must reconvene the IEP team to identify alternative strategies for meeting transition objectives if the agency that originally agreed to provide the services fails to do so.

Entitlement of BIA Schools to Benefits

BIA (Bureau of Indian Affairs) and tribally controlled schools are included in the Individuals With Disabilities Education Act. Services are available for Native Americans on reservations even if they are not BIA-funded. Students in BIA schools are entitled to the benefit of the EHA if they are qualified as students with disabilities.

Research Concerning SED Students

The secretary of education may conduct or make grants or contracts for studies concerning the education of students who are severely emotionally disturbed (SED).

Creation of Model Extended-School-Year Programs

The secretary of education may create model programs of extended school years, but the programs must integrate children with and without disabilities.

State Liability for Violation of This Act

Congress has made it clear that states are not immune from suit in federal court for violations of the EHA. Courts are allowed to award remedies in law and equity against a state that loses such a suit.

Provision of Early Education for Students With Disabilities

The amendment makes it clear that early education includes the education of the children's parents. It recommends that adult role models with disabilities be included as employees in early childhood programs, and it specifies that such programs should focus on the transition of infants and toddlers into early education and of young students from early education into elementary school. These programs should promote the use of assistive technology and address the early intervention and preschool needs of children exposed prenatally to maternal substance abuse.

Impact of the Individuals With Disabilities Education Act

There can be little doubt that the Individuals With Disabilities Education Act has had a great impact on the schools. The full impact, however, still cannot be assessed. The law is so new that many districts are still in the interpretation and implementation stages, and courts are working daily to define and specify the intent behind the terminology in the Act. Nevertheless, there is a body of case law that school districts may use to help answer their questions regarding what steps to take in order to comply with the law.

Case Law

The progress of individual students is one standard by which school districts' efforts to educate children with disabilities are judged. In *Polk* (*Polk v. Susquehanna I. E. U. No. 16*, 1988), the court held that there must be more than trivial progress in order to satisfy the *Rowley* standard of "opportunity for benefit" (*Hendrick Hudson District Board of Education v. Rowley*, 1982). In other words, it is expected that all students, regardless of the presence or absence of disabilities, will show such improvement as is possible given the nature and extent of their abilities.

Obviously then, a student who continues to fail and shows no improvement on standardized tests for a period of 3 years (*Hall v. Vance County Board of Education*, 1985), or a student who has regressed (*Board of Education of East Windsor Regional School District v. Diamond*, 1986), has not been provided an appropriate education.

In addition, courts will consider the individual student's particular situation. The careful formation and implementation of a proper IEP can do much to assure that the district will prevail if challenged. Cost may be considered in the planning of a student's IEP and in choosing among several alternatives (*Burke County Board of Education v. Denton*, 1990). Education in neighborhood schools is desirable but may not be required if an appropriate education can be provided elsewhere at less cost to the district (*Barnett v. Fairfax County School Board*, 1989). However, courts may order a remedy that impacts on state and local budgets (*Kerr Center Parents Association v. Charles*, 1990).

Students may be placed in programs outside of their local school or in separate programs within their local school when the extent of the disability is such that an appropriate education cannot be provided in a more integrated setting. Factors to be considered include the appropriateness of the separate program, costs to the district and effect on other students of accommodation in the regular program, unavailability of teachers, and findings of the LEA. Schools are not necessarily required to provide related services that are desirable if the student will benefit without them through the receipt of only necessary related services (*Rettiq v. Kent City School District*, 1983). Blanket policies are not individualized and do not meet the *Rowley* standard (*Zebley v. Sullivan*, 1990).

Parents are an important part of the process that decides on the best plan for educating children with disabilities. Their input should be sought and duly considered by the district, and their right to challenge the district's decisions should be respected. However, parents who interrupt or block the process required in *Rowley* for providing appropriate educational services to their child may not later claim that the process has not been satisfied (*Doe v. Defendant I*, 1990).

In the event of a challenge, the following points are relevant:

- In order to maintain order and safety in schools, students who physically threaten others at school, are disruptive, and damage property may be removed to a more restrictive placement during or prior to due process hearings (*Kurtz-Imig v. Township High School District Board of Education*, 1989).
- Parents are not required to notify the LEA prior to an independent evaluation of their child, in order to receive reimbursement for the evaluation. The LEA must show that their evaluation was appropriate in order to avoid paying.
- Compensatory education is a remedy for students when schools have failed to provide an appropriate placement within a reasonable time but not when the placement was appropriate but the student showed no progress (*Lester H. v. Carroll*, 1989).
- Minor procedural flaws that do not affect a student's ability to benefit do not violate the appropriate education rule (*Burke County Board of Education v. Denton*, 1990). If these flaws are found to affect this ability, however, they do violate the rule (*Spielberg v. Henrico County Public Schools*, 1987).
- A school is not required to pay nursing costs for care during school hours; however, Medicaid funding may be received for such services (*Detsel v. Board of Education*, 1987).

- Insurance companies may write policies that exclude EHA-reimbursable expenses (*Chester County Intermediate Unit v. Pennsylvania Blue Shield*, 1990).
- The deciding factor in determining who will pay for services and what services will be provided is the appropriate-education standard: If the services are necessary to provide an appropriate education, the LEA must pay for them; otherwise, it need not (*McClain v. Smith*, 1989). The services that are provided must address all of the student's needs and not just selected needs (*Rapid City School District 51-4 v. Vahle*, 1990). Per *Rowley*, maximum development is not required, only the opportunity to benefit. A certified special education teacher is not always required (*A. W. v. Northeast R-1 School District*, 1987). What is required is special considerations for students with special needs. Districts should take care not to let school rules overshadow school purpose. For example, most schools have rules prohibiting pets and other animals from being brought into their buildings. These rules are in place to increase student safety and enhance the orderliness of the educational environment—but a student may not be prohibited from bringing a service dog to school (*Sullivan v. Vallejo City Unified School District*, 1990).
- Districts should also be aware that the state's characterization of a facility (psychiatric or education-based) makes a difference to the courts in reviewing placement decisions. Factors considered are the nature of the program, setting, professional expertise of the workers, and necessity of the program to advance a student's education. Courts prefer to accept the judgment of state and local educational experts.

Where to Go for Help or Additional Information

The *Job Accommodation Network* (800-526-7234) is a valuable resource for schools that are trying to make reasonable accommodations without excessive costs. If demands are made for accommodations or inclusion of conditions that administrators believe are unreasonable, clarification of the law's requirements may be obtained through the *Office of the US Attorney General* at 202-514-0301 or the *EEOC* at 202-663-4903 (NASSP, 1992, February). The EEOC can also be reached at 800-USA-EEOC (Cape, 1992).

Rehabilitation Act of 1973: Recent Interpretations and Case Law

Purpose of the Statute

The section of the Rehabilitation Act of most interest to school administrators is Section 504, which prohibits discrimination against handicapped persons, including both students and staff members, by school districts receiving federal financial assistance. The directive includes all programs and activities of districts that are federally funded, regardless of whether the program in question is a direct recipient of such funding. It is Section 504 that requires that all students be provided with a free appropriate public education (FAPE) (Council of Administrators of Special Education [CASE], 1992).

Legislative Background

"The origins of Section 504 can be traced to World War I when proposals were raised in Congress to rehabilitate soldiers who received disabling injuries during the war" (Wenkart, 1990, p. 11).

The first legislation addressing these needs (and those of industrially disabled civilians) was enacted in 1920. It became part of the Social Security Act in 1935, and additional programs were enacted in 1943, 1954, 1965, 1967, and 1968. Although this legislation was a step forward, it was not reaching the population most in need of services, the severely disabled. The Rehabilitation Act of 1973 continued the attempt to serve the above populations and also addressed the needs of those who were more severely handicapped (Wenkart, 1990).

Major Provisions

Section 504 requires that otherwise qualified handicapped individuals not be excluded from participation in, be denied the benefits of, or be subjected to discrimination under any federally funded program or activity solely by reason of handicap. It means that possession of a handicap is not a permissible reason for assuming that an individual cannot function in a particular context. Decisions should be made individually based on actual abilities (Gordon, 1991).

To state a claim under Section 504, a plaintiff must prove the following: she or he is handicapped; she or he is otherwise qualified; she or he has been excluded solely by reason of the handicap; and the relevant program is receiving federal aid (Gordon, 1991).

Section 504 requires LEAs to provide a FAPE (including regular or special education and related aids and services that are designed to meet the individual student's needs) to each qualified handicapped child.

Section 504 defines handicapped students as those having any physical or mental impairment that substantially limits one or more major life activities (including learning). All handicapped students are protected regardless of whether they qualify for IDEA services or whether they require special education.

An evaluation is required for each student who may need special accommodations or related services under Section 504. If such evaluation determines that a student is handicapped, a plan for implementation and delivery of all needed services must be developed.

Districts should keep in mind the following:

1. The evaluation must be sufficient to accurately and completely assess the nature and extent of the handicap and the recommended services.
2. The determination of what services are needed must be made by a group of persons knowledgeable about the student.
3. Decisions about eligibility for services and/or what services are to be provided should be documented, placed in the student's file, and reviewed periodically.
4. Parents must be notified of any action affecting the identification, evaluation, or placement of their child. They are entitled to a hearing if they disagree with decisions made by the district. (CASE, 1992)

ADD/LEAs and Section 504

ADD and ADHD can result in significant learning problems for children with those conditions. Approximately 3%-5% of school-age children may be affected. Because ADD may qualify as a condition "which substantially limits a major life activity" (learning), if it is severe enough, children diagnosed with this handicap may qualify for services under Section 504. The LEA must evaluate any child believed to be handicapped by ADD. Districts identifying these children are responsible for providing special education and related services to them or for making any required adjustments in the identified children's regular classrooms.

SEAs and LEAs should take the necessary steps to promote coordination between special and regular education programs. Steps also should be taken to train regular education teachers and other personnel to develop their awareness about ADD and its manifestations and the adaptations that can be implemented in regular education programs to address the instructional needs of these children.

LEAs must have a system that allows parents to challenge district actions regarding the identification, evaluation, and placement of their child. This system must include notice, an opportunity for parents to examine records, an impartial hearing in which the parents may be represented by an attorney, and a review procedure.

Recent Cases

Though the settings in these cases were in higher education, the rulings apply to K-12 settings.

Grove City v. Bell (1984) was reversed by the Civil Rights Restoration Act of 1987. "The Act extends on an institution-wide basis and its reach is not limited to the specific program receiving federal aid" (Gordon, 1991 p. 11). This means that if one program violates a person's civil rights, the whole institution can be penalized.

In *Southeastern Community College v. Davis* (1979), the court defined an "otherwise qualified person" as one who can meet all of a program's requirements in spite of the handicap.

The *Wright v. Columbia University* (1981) court held that Section 504 prohibits paternalistic authorities from deciding that certain activities are too risky for a handicapped person.

In *Doherty v. Southern College of Optometry* (1988), the court ruled that an educational institution is not required to accommodate a handicapped individual by eliminating a course requirement that is reasonably necessary to proper use of the degree conferred at the end of the course of study.

Impact of the Rehabilitation Act

Because Section 504 is "a responsibility of the comprehensive general public education system," it is the responsibility of building administrators and superintendents of schools to see that it is implemented within their districts (CASE, 1992, p. 3).

Every public school in the nation is required to identify, evaluate, and provide appropriate services and procedural safeguards for handicapped students (CASE, 1992). (Note that under the later acts the preferred language is "persons with disabilities.")

Educational institutions are not required to make substantial modifications in programs to allow disabled persons to participate.

Florida has recently released a policy statement dealing with ADD. Students with ADD may fall under Section 504 if the disorder "substantially limits a major life activity." School districts are responsible for evaluating all students who may need special education and related services, including students diagnosed with ADD.

A school district's policy should include the following minimums:

- An affirmative statement that the district does not discriminate on the basis of handicap.
- Reference to Section 504 of the Rehabilitation Act of 1973.
- Reference to a referral/evaluation/placement process for students suspected of being handicapped under Section 504.

The Impact of Equal Access

The expanded equal access doctrine is summarized below:

1. The 1990 amendments to the Education of All Handicapped Children Act (now called the Individuals With Disabilities Education Act) make it clear that supported employment, use of assistive technology devices and services, full participation in community life, and integration into regular education programs for individuals with disabilities are high federal priorities.

2. The 1988 Technology-Related Assistance for Individuals With Disabilities Act funds statewide assistive technology programs in order to increase the independence, productivity, and integration of individuals with disabilities.

3. The 1986 amendments of the Rehabilitation Act created the supported employment initiative.

4. The 1986 and 1990 amendments to the Developmental Disabilities Assistance and Bill of Rights Act clarify that the purpose of the law is to help individuals with disabilities become independent, productive, and integrated into society.

5. The 1988 amendments to the Housing Act prohibit discrimination in housing.

6. The 1990 enactment of the Americans With Disabilities
   Act, PL 101-336, prohibits discrimination solely on the
   basis of disability in public accommodations, transportation, communications, and employment.

Schools will now be expected not only to provide education-
related services but to prepare students with disabilities to take full
advantage of services and opportunities in their post-secondary
school lives as well as to provide any transition services needed.

This doctrine is in quite a different spirit than the original. The
concept of equal access was established in 1973 in Section 504 of
the Rehabilitation Act. This law assumed that individuals with disabilities should have access to different resources for different purposes. Such individuals were thought to need different resources
because they would not be able to do the things nondisabled persons can do and would therefore have a life different from that of
nondisabled individuals (Turnbull, 1990).

The new equal access doctrine has a different set of assumptions.
"It means that individuals with disabilities should have equal access to different and the same resources for different and the same
results" (Turnbull, 1990, p. 5). In other words, some individuals
with disabilities will have the same kind of life as nondisabled individuals, and some will not. The kind of life and types of services,
programs, and activities in which an individual can participate de-
pends on the "extent of their disabilities, the degree to which society
accommodates them, personal choices of the disabled individual,
and the availability of support to meet their needs" (Turnbull,
1990, p. 28).

In order for this result to occur, "the doctrine assumes that equal
access to the same resources (including regular education) will
occur, with support. It also assumes that equal access to different
resources (such as special education) will occur, but for the purpose of enabling those with disabilities to have access to the 'nondisabled' or 'generic' world as well as to a world that is primarily
disability-oriented" (Turnbull, 1990, p. 26).

The following steps should be taken by school districts to help
ensure compliance with the Americans With Disabilities Act
(Long, n. d.):

1. Policies addressing key parts of Title 1 and Title 2 should be developed.
2. Information about the ADA's purpose and application to the school should be disseminated to interested individuals.
3. School personnel should be trained to understand and implement the requirements of the ADA.
4. Documentation should be kept regarding efforts to comply with the ADA.

Philosophies and Beliefs

Schools whose philosophies include a commitment to inclusive education share the following characteristics (Schattman & Benay, 1992):

1. There is a relationship between the inclusion approach and the broader issue of school reform.
   a. Schools making full use of inclusion are often engaged in other reform efforts.
   b. They often embrace well-articulated mission statements that reflect the values and beliefs of those involved in the school community.
   c. These mission statements speak to the needs of all children.
   d. Ongoing communication between interested parties is encouraged during formation of the mission statement.
2. Teaming approaches are used to create and implement programs and to address problems.
   a. The traditional one-teacher, one-classroom organization and its resultant isolation is broken—teachers, parents, and administrators are linked.
   b. Student-centered planning is considered essential.
   c. All parties are provided with a support network.
   d. The quality of outcomes is usually greater.
   e. Parents are involved in a meaningful way.
3. The roles of parents and educators change.
   a. Responsibility is shared among teachers, parents, and administrators.

    b. The parental role is elevated in importance.

    c. The teacher's role moves from specialist to generalist.

    d. Administrators no longer make unilateral decisions regarding the allocation of resources.

    e. The special education teacher moves from an isolated environment with limited contact with other teachers to a co-teacher role as part of each team.

4. Administrative roles in a team-based inclusive model also change. They include

    a. Challenging teams to make decisions that align with the mission and philosophy of their school.

    b. Modifying master schedules to support teachers with the time needed to meet as teams.

    c. Creating job descriptions that reflect the new roles of professionals working in a team-based system.

    d. Hiring personnel who embrace the district's philosophy and have appropriate technical and communication skills.

    e. Supervising and evaluating staff in a manner that supports the district's commitment to all children.

    f. Setting the agenda for staff meetings and including items that relate to support needs of all children.

    g. Arranging for inservice training for staff. (Schattman & Benay, 1992, p. 12)

Final Words to the School Administrator

"The ultimate goal of special education is to turn students into productive citizens." In order to be productive, students must be able to function in the workplace. Mainstreaming allows special education students to "develop the interpersonal skills necessary to survive in society [and] helps prepare the nondisabled for accepting workers with disabilities into the general workplace" (Osborne, 1992, p. 379).

Through statutes and court cases our national policy has now been set. We are on the road toward full integration of our citizens with disabilities into all aspects of our national life. Much of the burden, the promise, and the joy of this effort is in the hands of able and caring school administrators. Achieving integration of our children with disabilities is a large and visible segment of achieving integration for all persons with disabilities and of achieving the goal of justice for all our children.

Annotated Bibliography and References

Annotated Bibliography

Cape, L. M. (1992, July-August). The ADA in action: Protecting your right to work. *Arthritis Today*, pp. 49-50.

This article addresses the employment rights of arthritis sufferers and other persons with disabilities under the ADA. It is useful not only for those with arthritis but for persons with other physical disabilities as they seek employment. It would also be a helpful quick reference for personnel officers.

Collins, L. A., & Zirkel, P. A. (1992). To what extent, if any, may cost be a factor in special education cases? *Education Law Reporter, 71*, 11-25.

This article presents a circuit-by-circuit commentary on the extent to which cost may be considered in making special education placements. It is particularly useful for school administrators and special education directors who are facing difficult placement decisions and could also be a resource for parents of special needs children who may be questioning their student's placement.

Council of Administrators of Special Education, Inc. (CASE). (1992). *Student access: A resource guide for educators. Section 504 of the Rehabilitation Act of 1973.* Bloomington, IN: Author.

This handbook is provided by CASE to assist educators in interpreting and understanding Section 504 of the Rehabilitation Act. It is indexed and has an extensive table of contents, allowing educators to turn quickly to the section of most concern to them.

Coupe, B. W., Ness, A. D., & Sheetz, R. A. (1992). The Department of Justice's final regulations implementing Title III of the Americans With Disabilities Act. *Education Law Reporter, 71,* 353-359.

This commentary addresses what must be done by various agencies in order for them to be in compliance with the ADA. It gives a broad overview of the new regulations and how they may affect schools and other public institutions.

Gordon, J. I. (1991, January). *Issues related to disabled students and implementation of the Americans With Disabilities Act.* Paper presented at the 12th annual national conference on law and higher education. Stetson University College of Law, Clearwater Beach, FL.

This paper addresses the ADA's impact on students with disabilities. It is useful for teachers and administrators who need guidance regarding the treatment of students with disabilities in various situations.

Greismann, Z. (1990). Medically fragile children. *Education Law Reporter, 61,* 403-408.

This article presents an overview of case law surrounding the local education agency's responsibility to service medically fragile children in light of current legislation. The publication includes sections on the IDEA, the ADA, and Section 504 as well as discussions of court cases that address issues of interest to special educators.

Menacker, J. (1992). The "due weight" standard for special education hearing appeals. *Education Law Reporter, 73,* 11- 19.

This article offers a review of the due weight standard in special education hearing appeals. It includes a chart showing the conditions under which due weight will be applied. The chart is especially useful for administrators and special educators as they prepare individualized education plans or make placement decisions.

Miles, A. S., Russo, C. J., & Gordon, W. M. (1991). The reasonable accommodations provisions of the Americans With Disabilities Act. *Education Law Reporter, 69,* 1-8.

This article addresses the responsibilities that fall to public and private sector organizations in executing the reasonable accommodations provision of the ADA. School administrators will find this helpful as they design new facilities and programs under the ADA.

Osborne, A. G., Jr. (1990). When has a school district met its obligation to mainstream handicapped students under the EHA? *Education Law Reporter, 58,* 445-455.

This article presents a review of case law resulting from decisions on disputes about mainstreaming under the EHA. Administrators who find themselves with a difficult placement decision may find current case law helpful in determining the best course of action in their particular situation.

Osborne, A. G., Jr. (1992). The IDEA's least restrictive environment mandate: Implications for public policy. *Education Law Reporter, 71,* 369-380.

This commentary reviews recent court decisions surrounding special education placement disputes. Special attention is paid to decisions surrounding the selection of the least restrictive educational environment. Special educators, administrators, and others who are routinely involved in making placement decisions will find the instruction of the courts helpful in avoiding potential problems.

Parrino, S. S. (1992, July-August). A call to action. *Arthritis Today,* pp. 66-67.

This column informs arthritis sufferers of their legal rights under the ADA and urges them to stand up for themselves in discrimination cases. Others who suffer from various debilitating conditions may also find helpful information in the article, as will various advocacy groups.

Schattman, R., & Benay, J. (1992). Inclusive practices transform special education in the 1990s. *The School Administrator, 49*(2), 8-12.

This article traces the history of inclusive education and outlines present and future trends. Educational administrators who are reviewing or creating inclusive environments in their own schools may find suggestions that will lead to a smoother operation.

Turnbull, H. R. (1990). *Free appropriate public education* (3rd ed.). Denver, CO: Love.

This textbook addresses the history and present practices of courts, schools, and governments in providing a free appropriate public education to school children. It has extensive information on all facets of public education for students with disabilities and includes a large reference list.

Wenkart, R. D. (1990). The reasonable accommodation requirements of Section 504 of the Rehabilitation Act. *Education Law Reporter, 62,* 11-21.

This article presents an overview of the evolution of legislation and case law surrounding the reasonable accommodation provision of Section 504. Administrators who keep themselves informed of the direction of the courts can avoid a great many potential problems.

Zirkel, P. A. (1992). A special education case of parental hostility. *Education Law Reporter, 73,* 1-10.

This commentary addresses the courts' consideration of parental attitudes in special education placements. Both administrators and parents should be aware of the instruction of the courts regarding the amount of consideration that may be given to parental hostility and the conditions under which such consideration will be afforded.

References

A. W. v. Northeast R-1 School District, 813 F.2d 158 (8th Cir. 1987).

Alexander v. Choate, 469 U.S. 287 (1985).

Barlow/Gresham Union High School District No. 2 v. Mitchell, 16 EHLR 157 (D. Or. 1989).

Barnett v. Fairfax County School Board, 721 F. Supp. 757 (E.D. Va. 1989).

Begay v. Hodel, 730 F. Supp. 1001 (D. Ariz. 1990).

Board of Education of East Windsor Regional School District v. Diamond, 808 F.2d 987 (3rd Cir. 1986).

Briggs v. Board of Education of the State of Connecticut, 882 F.2d 688 (2d Cir. 1989).

Burke County Board of Education v. Denton, 895 F.2d 258 (4th Cir. 1990).

Burlington School Committee v. Massachusetts Department of Education, 736 F.2d 733 (1st Cir. 1984), aff'd, 471, U.S. 359 (1985).

Cape, L. M. (1992, July-August). The ADA in action: Protecting your right to work. *Arthritis Today*, pp. 49-50.

Carter v. Florence County School District Four, 950 F. 2d 156 (4th Cir. 1991), petition for cert. filed, 60 U.S.L.W. 3689 (U.S. Mar. 23, 1992) (No. 91-1523).

Chester County Intermediate Unit v. Pennsylvania Blue Shield, 896 F.2d 808 (3rd Cir. 1990).

Civil Rights Act of 1964, 42 U.S.C. section 200(d).

Council of Administrators of Special Education, Inc. (CASE). (1992). *Student access: A resource guide for educators. Section 504 of the Rehabilitation Act of 1973.* Bloomington IN: Author.

Daniels v. Williams, 474 U.S. 327 (1986).

Detsel v. Board of Education of the Auburn Enlarged City School District, 637 F.Supp. 1022 (N.D.N.Y. 1986), aff'd mem., 820 F.2d 587 (2d Cir.); cert. den., 484 U.S. 981, 108 S.Ct. 495, 98 L.Ed.3d 494 (1987).

Digre v. Independent School District No. 623, 893 F.2d 987 (8th Cir. 1990).

Doe v. Defendant I, 989 F.2d 1186 (6th Cir. 1990).

Doe v. Smith, 16 EHLR 65 (M.D. Tenn. 1988).

Doherty v. Southern College of Optometry, 659 F. Supp. 662, aff'd in part, rev'd in part, 862 F.2d 570, 1988 U.S. App. 16110 (1988).

E. H. v. Tirozzi, 735 F. Supp. 53 (D. Conn. 1990).

The Education For All Handicapped Children Act, P.L. 94-142, 20 U.S.C. at 1401 et seq. (1976), and the federal implementing regulations at 34 C.F.R. at 300.

Edward B. v. Paul, 814 F.2d 52 (1st Cir. 1987).

Ezratty v. Commonwealth of Puerto Rico, 648 F.2d 770 (1st Cir. 1983).

Gilette v. Fairland Board of Education, 725 F. Supp. 343 (S.D. Ohio 1989).

Gordon, J. I. (1991, January). *Issues related to disabled students and implementation of the Americans With Disabilities Act.* Paper presented at the 12th annual national conference on law and higher education. Stetson University College of Law, Clearwater Beach, FL.

Greismann, Z. (1990). Medically fragile children. *Education Law Reporter, 61*, 403-408.

Grove City v. Bell, 465 U.S. 555, 104 S.Ct. 1211, 79 L.Ed. 516 (1984).

Hall v. Vance County Board of Education, 774 F.2d 629 (4th Cir. 1985).

Harper v. School Administrative District No. 37, 727 F. Supp. 688 (D. Me. 1989).

Hendrick Hudson District Board of Education v. Rowley, 458 U.S. 176, 209, 102 S.Ct. 3034, 3052, 73 L.Ed.2d 690 (1982).

Irving Independent School District v. Tatro, 468 U.S. 883, 104 S.Ct. 3371, 82 L.Ed.2d 664 (1984).

J. G. v. Rochester City, 830 F.3d 447 (2d Cir. 1987).

Joseph P. v. Ambach, 669 F.2d 865 (2d Cir. 1982).

Kerr Center Parents Association v. Charles, 897 F.2d 1463 (9th Cir. 1990).

Kurtz-Imig v. Township High School District Board of Education, 16 EHLR 17 (N.D. Ill. 1989).

Lester H. v. Carroll, 16 EHLR 10 (E.D. Pa. 1989).

Lisio v. Woodland Hills School District, 734 F. Supp. 689 (W.D. Pa. 1989).

Long, K. L., (n. d.). *The Americans With Disabilities Act of 1990 and its impact on school districts.* Chalkboard. (Available from Rosenstein, Fist & Ringold, Third Floor, 525 S. Main, Tulsa, OK, 74103; Phone 918-585-9211.)

McClain v. Smith, 16 EHLR 6 (E.D. Tenn. 1989).

McKee, P. W., & Barbe, R. H. (1991). *The special educator 1991 desk book.* Horsham, PA: LRP.

Menacker, J. (1992). The "due weight" standard for special education hearing appeals. *Education Law Reporter, 73*, 11- 19.

Nathaniel L. v. Exeter School District, 16 EHLR 1073 (D.N.H. 1990).

National Association of Secondary School Principals (NASSP). (1992, February). The Americans With Disabilities Act. *Cases in Point*, p. 1.

Osborne, A. G., Jr. (1990). When has a school district met its obligation to mainstream handicapped students under the EHA? *Education Law Reporter, 58*, 445-455.

Osborne, A. G., Jr. (1992). The IDEA's least restrictive environment mandate: Implications for public policy. *Education Law Reporter, 71,* 369-380.

Parrino, S. S. (1992, July-August). A call to action. *Arthritis Today,* pp. 66-67.

Phipps v. New Hanover County Board of Education, 551 f. Supp. 732 (E.D. N.C. 1982).

Polk v. Susquehanna I.E.U. No. 16, 853 F.2d 171 (3rd Cir. 1988).

Public Law 101-336, U. S. Statutes at Large, 101st Congress, 2d Session, 1990. Vol. 104, Part 1, pp. 1-1016.

Rapid City School District 51-4 v. Vahle, 733 F. Supp. 1364 (D.S.D. 1990).

Rehabilitation Act (P.L. 93-112), 29 U.S.C. at 794 (1973), and the federal regulations for implementing the law at 34 C.F.R. at 104.

Rettig v. Kent City School District, 539 F. Supp. 768, aff'd in part, rev'd in part, 720 F.2d 466 (6th Cir. 1983).

Roncker v. Walter, 700 F.2d 1058 (6th Cir. 1983).

Schattman, R., & Benay, J. (1992). Inclusive practices transform special education in the 1990s. *The School Administrator, 49*(2), 8-12.

Southeastern Community College v. Davis, 442 U.S. 397, 60 L.Ed. 2d 980, 00 S.Ct. 2361 1979 U.S. Lexis 38 (1979).

Spielberg v. Henrico County Public Schools, EHLR 558:202 (E.D. Va. 1987).

Sullivan v. Vallejo City Unified School District, 731 F. Supp. 947 (E.D. Cal. 1990).

Tucker v. Bay Shore Union Free School District, 873 F.2d 563 (2d Cir. 1989).

Turnbull, H. R. (1990). *Free appropriate public education* (3rd ed.). Denver, CO: Love.

Webster Groves School District v. Pulitzer Publishing Company, 898 F.2d 1371 (8th Cir. 1990).

Wenkart, R. D. (1990). The reasonable accommodation requirements of Section 504 of the Rehabilitation Act. *Education Law Reporter, 62,* 11-21.

Wright v. Columbia University, 520 F. Supp. 789 (1981).

Zebly v. Sullivan, 16 EHLR 438 (U.S. 1990)

Zirkel, P. A. (1992). A special education case of parental hostility. *Education Law Reporter, 73,* 1-10.